How To Become a Veterinarian

Zachary Patterson, DVM

DEDICATION

To my wife Melissa, my best friend and love of my life, and
my children, Aliceyn & Benson

CONTENTS

ACKNOWLEDGMENTS

This book would not have been possible without the contributions and support of so many in me becoming a veterinarian and in the production of the book itself. Thanks go out to my sisters, parents, and grandparents for providing me encouragement and support along the way.

I would also like to express gratitude to Dr. R.C. Ebert, Dr. Ronald Baker, Dr. Douglas Hardy, Dr. Lois Davis, Dr. Jonathan Blake and the many other veterinarians who have provided me with invaluable guidance and mentorship over the years. I also am very appreciative of the efforts of (future Dr.) Sofia Miele for editing and providing additional perspective for the book.

Finally, my most sincere thanks goes to my wife and children, who have been my companions every step of the way. Simple words cannot express my gratitude for the sacrifices that each of you have made to make this life for ourselves.

So You Want to Be a Veterinarian?

There are so many reasons to be a veterinarian. Aside from my interest in science and caring for animals, a big draw for me to this profession was how respected and revered veterinarians are in their communities. Veterinarians are consistently near the top of the list of most trusted and respected professionals in just about any opinion poll. In addition to being able to do a job you love, you also have the option of being your own "boss". I found the idea of someday being able to run my own business very attractive, but this is just one of the many options that exist in the veterinary profession.

Veterinarians are afforded the opportunity to do so many different things with their knowledge and skills. When most people think about veterinarians, the veterinarian in the office down the street probably comes to mind. This is referred to as a "general practitioner" in our field. However, a Doctor of Veterinary Medicine (DVM) degree allows you to do almost anything, from researching new medical technologies and developing the cures of tomorrow, to ensuring the safety of food products, or even developing the next generation of minds as a professor or instructor.

Additional training after veterinary school opens up even more possibilities. A veterinarian can specialize in just about any field. Specialties in small animals include surgery, internal medicine, cardiology, neurology, emergency medicine, oncology, dentistry, anesthesiology, ophthalmology, and exotic animal medicine. If you prefer to work with large animals, specialties exist in equine medicine and surgery as well as food animal medicine and surgery. This is a very incomplete list, as the possibilities are virtually limitless.

You are probably reading this book because you or someone close to you (child, grandchild, niece, nephew, etc.) has an interest in becoming a veterinarian. As a veterinarian, a major contributor to my job satisfaction is hearing from young people with these aspirations. It warms my heart every time I see an interested and wide eyed child who comes in with the family pet and exclaims "I want to be a veterinarian!" Becoming a veterinarian is consistently one of the most popular "When I Grow Up" dreams among children and teens. This means I get to meet enthusiastic kids all the time, but this is also the main reason why becoming a veterinarian is highly competitive.

That's not to say it can't be done, or isn't within the reach of every interested child. All it takes is hard work and determination, and most importantly, a plan. The intent of this book is to guide you through the process of getting into veterinary school and becoming a veterinarian. Reading this book represents the starting point in developing your plan to realize this dream. Believe me, in the end, all the time, effort, and money spent on pursuing this dream will be worth it. You can't put a price on getting to do what you love on a daily basis. I wake up every morning looking forward to "work". I consider myself very fortunate to be a member of this profession, and just about every one of my colleagues would agree. Congratulations on taking your first step on the path to becoming a veterinarian.

Ways to get into Vet School

Before we jump to what you need to do to become a veterinarian, let's briefly discuss the two most common routes to get into veterinary school: By Application or a Guaranteed Acceptance Program.

The Application Process is the way that most people are familiar with, because it is still the most common way by which students enter a veterinary program. Candidates submit an application to the veterinary school(s) of their choice; these applications are evaluated by the admissions committee and worthy individuals are selected for interviews. Those interviewed are then considered and ranked based on a variety of factors. These rankings are then used to fill the open spots in the class for the upcoming fall. The top individuals remaining are placed on a waiting list, while the rest are notified that they were not accepted. Veterinary school is highly competitive, for every student accepted, several others are not. We will devote an entire chapter to the application process later; this brief overview was done to give context to some of the points made in ensuing chapters.

Guaranteed Acceptance programs exist at most veterinary schools. These programs award high achieving high school students guaranteed acceptance to veterinary school if they continue to meet certain standards during their undergraduate education. Some programs require completing a certain bachelor's degree program (such as animal science or biology). Others allow for guaranteed early acceptance after completing the minimum requirements for application to veterinary school. This can be as little as 60 college credit hours. I know several individuals who started veterinary school at age 20, with just two years of college course work. Regardless of the timeline for the program, other stipulations are put in place, such as college GPA requirements, and minimum course load (hours taken per semester). These additional requirements ensure that the students continue their track record of high academic performance through college into veterinary school.

These programs are extremely competitive and/or have high minimum standards such as an excellent high school GPA and class rank, usually in the top 10% of your graduating class or better. A high score on the ACT or SAT is also usually required. Minimum requirements vary by school, but most programs require a 27-30 on the ACT or 1220-1340 on the SAT. If getting into one of these programs is your goal, be sure to pay close attention in the next section for how to best position yourself in high school for success.

It starts in High School

Don't get me wrong, you don't have to start your journey in High School, or before. I went to Veterinary school with many people who had taken different paths to get there. Some had served in the military, or worked in other careers for several years before going back to school to become veterinarians. While most of my classmates were in their early to mid-twenties, some were in their thirties, even their late thirties.

However, the most common route and the most direct way to realizing your dream is to gain acceptance to veterinary school directly after finishing your undergraduate work. There are several ways to improve your chances or even guarantee acceptance into veterinary school based on your performance in high school. Also, veterinary school is very expensive; when added to undergraduate student debt, you could end up borrowing a lot of money. Doing well in high school could help you land scholarships that will cover some or all of your undergraduate education expenses. I cannot understate this point enough; many veterinary school graduates (myself included) literally owe more money in student loan debt than their home mortgage. I know some couples who met in veterinary school and later married that owe over $300,000 combined! It can be crippling. I will frequently come back to this point, and describe ways to reduce the debt load you incur during your journey.

In this chapter, we will discuss grades, standardized tests, extra-curricular activities, course selections, and set goals that will best position you for college and veterinary school.

Grades are, as you might suspect, an important part of the equation. Your grades in high school will have little to no direct bearing on whether or not you get into veterinary school, but they are still extremely important. Almost every college scholarship out there on some level considers your grades, or lists a specific grade point average (GPA) or class rank as a minimum requirement. Additionally, standardized college admissions exams such as the SAT or ACT are based on the high school college preparatory curriculum.

The best way to prepare for the SAT or ACT is not to cram for the test or go to a special training course outside of school. Those things may help, but mastering the subjects you are exposed to on a daily basis at school is the best way to build the knowledge base to score well on those tests. Grades also are an important qualifier if you would like to be considered for a guaranteed acceptance program as we discussed earlier. Do as well as you can in high school and work to develop good study habits during this time. They will come in very handy in college and especially veterinary school.

Standardized tests such as the ACT or SAT are major factors that colleges consider when evaluating high school students. The way most college admissions and scholarship criteria are set up, a student's ACT or SAT can carry about as much weight as their overall GPA. A GPA is based on performance over four years, the other (SAT/ACT) based on performance during a 4 hour test.

As discussed earlier, mastering daily classroom work is the best way to build the knowledge base required to score well on these tests. However, at home preparatory courses either on the computer or in book form can definitely help by exposing you to some of the emphasized principles on these tests and sample questions. Learning centers also typically offer courses in the evenings and on weekends for several weeks or months leading up to the exam. These can also really help; I have known students that increased their scores significantly by completing one of these courses.

A factor many students and parents don't consider when it comes to the ACT and SAT is timing. Depending on which courses they have taken, most students have been exposed to most, if not all, of the material on the SAT or ACT by the end of their junior year of high school. This is also the year in which many students get their best score. Also, most colleges have deadlines for admissions or scholarship applications which are early in a student's senior year. These deadlines do not allow the student time to submit scores from tests taken later in their senior year.

All these factors show that a student should strive to achieve the best possible score by the end of their junior year. In order to be best prepared for test dates during their junior year, it only makes sense that the student would not be taking the test for the first time. Taking these exams at least once during the sophomore year (10th grade) gets all those first time jitters and anxiety out of the way. Time management and pace are extremely important on these tests and many students do not finish every section in the time allowed. These tests are also very fatiguing; your brain may feel totally cooked at the end of the day (I know mine was). Having the experience of taking the test before allows you to troubleshoot and plan for future attempts. And who knows you may get your best score or meet your test score goal(s) on your first try. Many students do just that, and don't have to worry about taking either test again!

Testing during the summer break is not recommended, as having even a couple of weeks away from school seems to really effect how engaged the students' mind is. I know I felt like I was less sharp the time I took the ACT during the summer.

Extra-curricular Activities in high school might not seem all that important, but they are key for a number of different reasons. Colleges like to see a variety of extracurricular activities to show that a student is well-rounded. Extracurricular activities are also examined by scholarship selection committees. These committees are given the difficult task of choosing among students who all have strong academic profiles that are often very similar if not essentially identical. Extracurricular activities can be what helps cast the deciding vote between equally qualified applicants.

Every school district offers a wide variety of clubs, student organizations, athletic teams, and musical activities that will fit any talent or interest. Don't overextend yourself, extracurricular activities should not come at the expense of performance in the classroom, but there should be plenty of time for a good balance between the two. I encourage you to take a leadership role in these activities as well; being able to list that you were President of an organization or Team Captain illustrates dependability, initiative, and respect among peers to those evaluating you. Some specific clubs to consider are Future Farmers of America (FFA) and 4-H. These organizations provide students with additional opportunities to gain knowledge and experience with a variety of animal species. 4-H even offers a Veterinary Science curriculum.

A high priority during the High School years should also be placed on obtaining a significant number of hours of veterinary experience. Priority should be place on gaining direct experience by closely observing the practice of veterinary medicine, such as observing surgeries, procedures, or physical exams. Time spent performing some common tasks around a veterinary clinic such as cleaning kennels, stocking supplies, and other menial tasks still count as veterinary experience and will provide value to you in the future as well.

General animal experience is also looked upon favorably by veterinary school admissions committees and is defined as animal-related work that was not performed under the supervision of a veterinarian. Veterinary experience is preferable, but don't turn down a good opportunity to earn hours in either category. All hours should be tracked and recorded. We will go over tabulating these hours in the "Getting into Vet School" chapter when we cover the veterinary school application process.

The number of hours of experience a student has obtained can play a big role in whether or not they are accepted into veterinary school. Most schools have a minimum number of hours that all candidates must have, but the majority of students that are accepted greatly exceed the minimum requirement, and often have thousands of hours of experience.

Veterinary schools still train students in both Large and Small animal medicine, so it is critical to gain experience by observing veterinarians working with a variety of species, especially Dogs, Cats, Horses, and Cattle. Additional experience with Exotic animals, animal research, and animal shelters is helpful as well, and may even set you apart from other applicants. There will be an opportunity to gain this experience during college, but it may be difficult to reach the target number of hours during college alone.

There are two ways that most students accrue veterinary experience: as a volunteer or as an employee of a veterinary practice. There are positives and negatives to both. Working as a volunteer allows more flexibility to how and when you gain observation hours. You often set the schedule or just show up when you can. Being a volunteer also means that the clinic is not counting on you to accomplish a specific set of tasks. You are essentially extra help, so a higher percentage of your time may be spent directly observing a veterinarian on the job.

However, as a volunteer, you may not be allowed to participate in very much hands-on experience as many practices have a policy to avoid putting individuals that are not on the payroll at risk of injury because they are not protected by workman's compensation and other insurance provisions. Also, without being required to work specific shifts, you may end up logging less observation time. This depends on the individuals' initiative and willingness to choose to accrue volunteer hours over doing other things that might be more fun. This may be a tough choice to make at times.

As an employee of a veterinary practice, you get paid to work at the clinic while gaining observation time as well. Most clinics are very good about understanding that you are working there to gain this experience and have a job description that affords you the opportunity to spend as much time as possible directly observing and working with veterinarians. However, the practice may still require completion of other tasks during work shifts such as cleaning kennels, stocking veterinary supplies, taking inventory, stocking the farm call truck, etc.

Unfortunately some clinics give too many of these responsibilities to a shadowing employee, causing them to spend the majority of their shifts doing these tasks rather than gaining experience. This is a situation to avoid. Try asking previous pre-veterinary employees about their experience before taking a job. If this is a problem you discover after starting a job, try discussing the issue with the practice. They may not realize that this is an issue and that your expectations for gaining experience are not being met.

Many students are accepted into vet school with most or even all of their experience being as an unpaid volunteer. This may be a better fit for some individuals, but I would recommend that students seek to gain employment at a veterinary practice. I believe it affords the best opportunity to gain a significant amount of high quality hours experience and earn some money at the same time. It is a very efficient use of time (which is at a premium) and can also lead to a possible job opportunity in the future as your work ethic and attitude may be more readily on display. I don't see much of the drawback of potentially spending some of those hours performing general labor. Knowledge of all of the different tasks and responsibilities that are essential to making a hospital run properly is important to a veterinarian who also often functions as a manager of the practice employees. If you don't know what needs to be done, how are you supposed to make sure key tasks are being accomplished?

Course selections made in high school are vital to getting on the right path academically. College admission tests such as the ACT and SAT reward students who excel in all areas, so students should seek the highest level of instruction in the core subjects of English, Reading Comprehension, Math, and Science. However, as you will see later, students will also be required to complete multiple college courses on Physics, Chemistry, and Biology.

Accordingly, it is important that students establish a strong base in these subjects in high school if possible. This generally means that students will be taking some science courses as their electives since most schools only require 3 or 4 science classes. It can be tough having to take an extra year of chemistry or biology instead of that fun photography class, but keeping the focus on achieving the ultimate goal of becoming a veterinarian should take precedence, and sacrifices big and small must be made along the way.

The benefit of taking advanced courses in the sciences is that they can open up opportunities to earn college credit in high school. These are often referred to as dual credit courses as the student earns both high school and college credit. Getting some of these classes out of the way can ease the workload in college, allow the student to apply to vet school early or graduate ahead of schedule. Seeking a high level of instruction in English and Math can afford similar opportunities for college credit. I met the math requirement for applying to veterinary school by taking college algebra as a high school senior.

The number of dual credit courses available varies from school to school, but I know many students who were able to earn 30 college credit hours or more in high school, which is a year of college credit at the standard load of 15 credit hours per semester. This allowed these students to apply and be accepted into veterinary school at age 20 after just two years of undergraduate college work. However, most students had three or more years of college.

Clearly, earning college credit in high school can pay big dividends, and in addition to dual credit courses, even more classes can be taken in the evenings, weekends, or summer breaks at local colleges. This is not utilized by many students, and I understand why. What high school student wants to spend more time in the classroom than they have to? However, taking a class at a local community college or similar institution is another source of inexpensive college credits with courses that can be a bit easier than their counterparts at universities.

My school didn't offer a large number of dual credit courses, so I took my college speech class on Monday nights my senior year of high school. I even think there was a local scholarship that covered the entire cost. There may be a similar scholarship out there for you, and there is probably very little competition for it. Check with your school's counselor or college advisor and contact the local community college(s) to find out about these scholarship opportunities.

Outside of the core subjects, elective courses in the agriculture department such as animal science, livestock production, equine health, or general veterinary science can also be beneficial, especially if the student does not have much of a farm background. This will show that you are making the effort to become a well-rounded student. Not only does it demonstrate initiative, but it also shows you understand and recognize the importance of all aspects of veterinary medicine.

Finally, I would recommend trying to fit a study hall into your schedule when possible. Having a busy extra-curricular schedule can make it difficult to get all assignments or studying done outside of school. That extra hour during the day for studying or homework can be very helpful. Finding a schedule spot for the study hall should not come at the expense of scheduling one of the more important core subject classes listed above, however.

Setting goals is very important along the way. Start with smaller, short term targets, like doing well in a particular class or during a semester, and work up to larger accomplishments such as obtaining a significant scholarship, ranking at or near the top of your graduating class, or being chosen for a guaranteed veterinary school acceptance program. Successfully achieving your smaller goals keeps you on track for reaching the larger ones.

The goals are going to vary somewhat from person to person, but by the time a student starts college, they should strive to have gained at least 1,000 hours of veterinary experience, a strong background in the sciences, and shown a track record of academic success in the classroom and on standardized tests. Developing and working on these goals provide a clear sense of structure and direction as you move along in your journey to becoming a veterinarian.

Picking the Right College or University

It can seem quite daunting to pick the right college or university. There are literally thousands of options out there. Narrowing them down to a short list of possibilities can be an exhausting task, especially if there are not clear factors by which you base the decision to eliminate or include schools on your list. In this chapter, I will discuss factors to consider when selecting THE school that will best position a pre-veterinary student for being accepted into veterinary school.

The first school(s) to make the short list should be in-state universities that that have a veterinary school. These schools are generally large state universities or private schools. As of 2013, there were 28 veterinary schools in the United States, with several new schools in the planning or development phase that could open in the next several years. These colleges and universities with veterinary schools offer some advantages. First, they usually have a very prominent pre-veterinary program, as there are usually a lot of students at these schools who also seek to become veterinarians.

As a result, there is often more structure in place for those students interested in veterinary medicine, with faculty advisors who specifically work with pre-veterinary students. The pre-veterinary clubs at these schools are usually very active and can be quite large. There may even be special course offerings that are associated with the veterinary school for undergraduate students. These courses can help students develop a stronger pre-veterinary background.

Additional in-state colleges and universities that don't have veterinary schools should be added if they have strong biology or animal science programs that have a track record of helping students continue on to veterinary school. These schools generally also have a solid pre-veterinary club and faculty advisors that know how to best position pre-veterinary students for successful veterinary school applications. It doesn't hurt if these faculty advisors are veterinarians or have other connections to some veterinary schools, as their recommendation letters can be invaluable.

At this point, you might be asking why the preference for in-state options? The reason why I give priority to in-state schools is that these institutions generally offer in-state students reduced tuition costs, often times 50% less than what out of state students pay in tuition and fees. This applies to both undergraduate costs and veterinary school. Over the course of undergraduate training and veterinary school, this price break for in-state tuition can really add up to well over $100,000 or more. As I emphasized earlier, the cost of becoming a veterinarian should be kept to a minimum. Such a significant savings opportunity, in my opinion, is simply too good to pass up.

I understand wanting to branch out and go to a school hundreds or even thousands of miles away. If you can do this while incurring little to no student loan debt by qualifying scholarships, financial aid, or with the financial support of family members, I encourage you to take the opportunity such a move presents for personal growth. However, most people feel about the same amount of independence being several hours away as they would if they were 2,000 miles away from home.

If you are set on choosing an out of state institution, try to find one that meets the same criteria in the two paragraphs above that also has a relaxed policy on obtaining residence in that state with easy to meet criteria. I know my alma-mater, the University of Missouri, has one of the most relaxed policies. Students were able to become Missouri residents and get the in-state tuition rates within one year by meeting basic requirements such as registering to vote, getting a Missouri driver's license, and working a part-time job a certain number of hours through the course of the year. I know several out of state students who said this was a major deciding factor for where they would attend school. In most states, however, it is very difficult to obtain residency while attending a school within that state. This should be examined closely on a case by case basis when you are developing your list of college choices.

You should now have a broad list of options which may need to be narrowed down further, or maybe the list is short enough, but you need to rank the schools on it. Your list of schools should be short enough so that you can visit each one for a day or two to both tour campus and meet with potential faculty advisors. There are many different factors you will consider when paring down your list of potential colleges to a manageable number or when ranking them and selecting the best fit. However, there are some factors that are particularly relevant to becoming a veterinarian and your long term success. Particularly, scholarship offerings, overall cost of attendance, and a track record of pre-veterinary student success.

Scholarships: Hopefully you were able to meet your goals in high school and have positioned yourself well for a variety of scholarship opportunities. These can be academic or through your extracurricular activities such as athletics, the arts and music, or various clubs. The scholarships offered by each college and university should be reviewed closely.

Colleges offering better scholarship packages for which you are eligible should receive priority. Pay particular attention to the eligibility requirements such as class rank, GPA, and minimum ACT or SAT score. Also note if there is an unlimited number of each scholarship available or if the scholarship is granted to a certain number of applicants. If it is limited, find out how they select the recipients from the pool of eligible candidates and the number of students that typically apply for that scholarship each year. The highest paying scholarships are often limited to a specific number of students, and obtaining answers to these questions will allow you to gauge your odds of being selected. If they give 200 scholarships, but 2,000 high achieving, equally qualified students apply, it may be difficult to count on being selected.

However, there is usually a nice "consolation prize" sort of scholarship that may be almost as good. This was the case for me. I was not selected for the equivalent of a full ride scholarship at the university I chose to attend which would have covered tuition and the cost to live on campus. Those of us who were not selected received the next best scholarship, which was awarded to an unlimited number of qualifying students and it covered all tuition costs. Having free room and board would have been nice, however, many students (myself included) prefer to live off campus, so missing out on that part of the scholarship was not a total loss.

If you have a great talent in athletics, music, or the performing arts you may be eligible for a scholarship in one of these areas. A significant time commitment can be required of student athletes as well as those in the arts. Be sure you will still be able to balance your time with positioning yourself well to get into vet school by taking a challenging and full (15+ credit hrs.) course load and gaining further veterinary experience. I had several veterinary school classmates who had been student athletes who compared it to being similar to maintaining a full time job most of the school year. They are a testament to the fact that it can be done, but the time commitment should be considered at length.

Each school may also offer scholarships for students entering majors in a specific department. Check with the departments of the majors you are interested to see if you are eligible. Finally, clubs and organizations you are involved with in High School may offer scholarships as well. It is important to seek out and apply for any scholarship opportunity available to minimize the cost of your undergraduate education to keep the total cost of your education as a whole as low as possible. Therefore, scholarship opportunities should be an important deciding factor when choosing a college or university.

Overall Cost of Attendance: In keeping with the central theme of minimizing your student loan debt load, the cost of attendance of each college should be reviewed closely. Obvious things to look at are the costs for tuition and fees for each year based on a 15 credit hour per semester workload. Sometimes the tuition will be reasonable, but additional fees charged to help pay for the new nice student union or recreational center can really add up.

Housing and food costs also factor into the total cost of attendance. Compare the costs of living on campus with living off campus. If you have the option of living off campus, you can often decrease the cost of room and board by living with roommates. However this may not be true in parts of the country where real estate is expensive, such as the west coast or the northeast. Costs for basic needs such as food, clothing, gas, and utilities can also vary widely depending on what city or region the school is located. The best value may be to live on campus or avoid colleges in cities with a high cost of living altogether.

Track Record of Pre-Veterinary Student Success:
Colleges and Universities that have veterinary schools are going to have a solid advantage here, by pure nature that a significant portion of students accepted to those veterinary schools are coming from their own undergraduate pre-veterinary student pool. As mentioned earlier, these schools generally have a large and well-established pre-veterinary program with several faculty advisors that focus on or work exclusively with pre-veterinary students. In addition, there is usually an active pre-veterinary club and there may be special veterinary course offerings for undergraduate students that you might not find elsewhere.

However, there are some potential disadvantages of being a member of such a large pre-veterinary population. It may be difficult to schedule certain courses because of the large demand or to stand out among your peers in such a large group. It can also be difficult to find quality opportunities to further build your veterinary experience. The typical small to medium sized college town will only have a finite number of veterinary clinics, and the demand for jobs or volunteer hours could greatly outpace the supply. All things considered, colleges or universities that have a veterinary school offer a very good, if not the best environment for fostering student success and aiding in their progress to getting accepted into veterinary school and should receive strong consideration from any student desiring to become a veterinarian. They are not, however, the only schools you should consider.

There are many other schools that have a strong record of pre-veterinary student success that do not have a veterinary school as part of their campus. These schools may not have as many students in their pre-veterinary program or as many veterinary-based courses for undergraduate students, but they can still provide an excellent environment for becoming a veterinarian. Probably 50% or more of veterinary students attend a different institution for their undergraduate work before moving on to veterinary school. There may not be as much competition for quality veterinary experience opportunities in the local area with a smaller number of pre-veterinary students at the school and you could find it easier to stand out among your peers in classes. Also, veterinary-related classes may be easier to get into or might have fewer students in them, allowing for more individual attention from professors.

The trouble is in determining which institutions fit the description above. This may take a little work on your part, but after doing your research, you might determine that one of these schools is the best fit for you. The first place to look for information is at veterinary school websites. If there is a veterinary school in your state or specific veterinary schools that accept the most students from your state start there. Schools will often publish information about each incoming class such as demographics, GPA, etc. Sometimes they will also list the schools from which students were selected from. If this information is not available online, try contacting the veterinary school, they may have the information you seek. If students are consistently getting accepted from a certain college or university, chances are it is a good environment for academic and personal growth for pre-veterinary students.

Contacting student advisors at prospective universities can also be very informative. Specifically focus on their experience with pre-veterinary students and try to determine if they have potential connections to veterinary school(s) or are well known. Having recommendation letters from an advisor with these credentials can give your veterinary school application a huge boost. Just keep in mind that you still have to actually earn the recommendation!

After gathering and considering all the information and visiting the schools on your "short list", you have to choose which one is the right school for you. I certainly hope the decision is very easy and clear cut for you, but if it isn't, don't make the decision in haste. Starting your research process early will allow you more time to consider your options and to make the most informed decision possible. I recommend students start looking at college options their sophomore year of high school, and have their short list of schools by the end of their junior year. This allows the student to make visits to prospective schools over the summer break prior to the senior year.

The College Years

College is often reflected upon as a golden age of sorts for most people, and for good reason. It is the time of becoming an adult, forging tons of new relationships, and growing both personally and intellectually. There are so many new opportunities and experiences that you will have access to. Truly enjoy these times. Like your high school years, college only takes up a relatively small segment of your life. Take it all in, responsibly of course. Be sure to keep your eye on the prize of becoming a veterinarian and maintain your focus on this goal. There is plenty of room for both enjoying this time while still accomplishing the tasks and milestones necessary to best position yourself for applying to veterinary school.

In this chapter, we will cover choosing a major, grades, course selections, extra-curricular activities and set benchmarks to give you every advantage heading into the veterinary school application process.

Choosing a Major: This may not be as difficult of a task for you compared to some of your peers who aren't sure of their career choice. You, however, seek to become a veterinarian, which naturally pushes you towards majors in Animal Science, Biology, Chemistry, and other related fields. These majors often have many, if not all of the required courses for veterinary school admission built into their program or facilitate their inclusion as electives. The overwhelming majority of students entering veterinary school come from one of these majors.

However, there is not a requirement for a specific major, just requirements of specific courses, so you can major in anything you choose so long as you take the required courses for veterinary school admission along the way. I know students who had degrees in business, the arts, or the humanities who went on to become veterinarians. In fact, I would argue that choosing an unrelated major is the right choice under certain circumstances.

The first step in choosing a major is deciding what you will fall back on in the event you are not able to become a veterinarian. I don't like mentioning this scenario because I don't want thoughts of not succeeding in your dream to be on your mind at all; fear of failure can be self-fulfilling. Do not fear this possibility, but it would also be naïve to avoid acknowledging its existence. There are scores of well qualified students who are not accepted into veterinary school every year. Many, if not all of these individuals would make good veterinarians. I want you to overcome any fear or anxiety you might have about not achieving your goal by confronting it head on. Accept it as a possibility and make peace with it. At the end of the day, if you have given your best effort, but you come up short, that is not something to be disappointed in or ashamed of.

A key to this process is identifying the vocation that is the next best thing for you. You may not be as strongly attached to it as being a veterinarian, but hopefully there is one or even several other things you would be *almost* as happy doing for the rest of your life. I felt empowered by the fact that I had several other aspirations that I felt this way about. I could even see some scenarios where I would be just as happy as being a veterinarian. For example, I could see myself working in sports journalism, as a lawyer, or in the ethanol/brewing industry. So even if things didn't work out for me trying to become a veterinarian, I had identified alternatives and had a plan of action in place. This sense of security allowed me to push any fear out of my mind and keep it out of the way of my success. By doing this, you can move forward with the confidence that regardless of what happens, you're going to be just fine.

After determining your fallback option(s) consider how it fits with your primary goal of becoming a veterinarian. Choosing a major is easy if your fallback option is in a related field, and requires a degree in Animal Science, Biology, or Chemistry. Where it can get difficult is if your second dream is in a completely different field. It is difficult to major in a vastly different department such as business, journalism, or the arts and also fit in all the required courses for veterinary school while graduating on time or getting yourself into position to for early application to veterinary school. This is where your priorities come into place, and you have to make a decision after weighing your various options against your goals and desires.

Interests, goals, and aspirations will vary from person to person, so I can't provide specific guidance to your situation. I feel that my personal experience was not unique and the decision-making process that I used can be made applicable to just about anyone. My main goal was to be accepted to veterinary school early. I did not have the opportunity to earn enough college credit in high school to be able to get into veterinary school after just two years, but three years was a very attainable goal. After considering this primary goal with my fallback options, the best choice for me was a major in biology, specifically organismal biology.

All of the courses required for veterinary school were built into my major, and with this major, I could work in the ethanol or brewing industry, which was one of my fallback careers. This major allowed me to be on track to apply to veterinary school as a college junior and if I was not accepted after applying both my junior and senior years of college, I would still graduate on time (4 years), and be able to enter the workforce in another field of work that I felt I would be very happy with.

As I alluded to earlier, you may find that the best choice for you is a major in a completely unrelated area. If that is what fits your goals and interests the best, then it is the right decision. Carefully considering your priorities and thinking through all of your options will lead you to the right choice for your major.

Grades in your college courses are probably the most important factor in getting into veterinary school. That doesn't mean you should place too much pressure on yourself, but grades are very critical and can make or break your application. College can be a lot of fun, and definitely enjoy this time, but also be sure to maintain your focus. In the classroom, strive to do your best and gain a solid educational base, particularly in the sciences. Standardized tests such as the MCAT and the GRE are based on information covered in the undergraduate curriculum. You don't have to make straight A's but the way to maximize your chances of admission is to achieve as high of a GPA as possible.

Depending on the school(s) you will apply to, your overall GPA may not be the only number that matters. Many Veterinary schools specifically look at your GPA in science courses and place some weight on this number in comparison to your overall GPA. Some also look the GPA from your last 2 or 3 semesters of work, where most students are taking higher level courses. They see these higher level courses as most comparable to the courses you will take in veterinary school, and students excelling in these higher level courses may be more likely to do well in veterinary school. We will cover this more when we set goals to strive for during college to put you in the best position possible for the veterinary school application process.

Course Selections can be critical in a number of ways. You will have a list of courses that are required for veterinary school and/or your major, but the order in which you take them is important. Obtaining the right mix of courses each semester can be very helpful in allowing you to make the best grades possible. Most undergraduate programs are designed so that most if not all of the general education courses are taken during the freshmen and sophomore years.

Courses in the sciences often build off one another or a base in a subject consisting of one or more courses are required before a wider selection of courses in that subject will be available to you. For example, you may have to take a sequence in chemistry similar to this one: Chemistry I -> Chemistry II -> Organic Chemistry ->Biochemistry. This structure would only allow you to take one chemistry class at a time (not that you would normally want to take more than one, we will get to why soon) The biology department may require a base in the subject developed by requiring all students to take Biology I and then Biology II before you can move on to other courses such as Genetics, Microbiology, Physiology, and Anatomy.

My point is that it may be difficult to schedule a lot of your science courses early on, and you probably don't want to have an overly difficult schedule your first couple of semesters. However, you also don't want to skimp on them and have to load up later. While you may not find that all of your science classes are difficult, they are likely to be more challenging than general education courses or some of your electives. You should seek to have roughly 2-3 of your courses every semester to be from this group of more challenging courses in math and science.

Knowing an upper classmen who has taken these classes before can be very helpful in identifying which ones will be more difficult than others. They can also give insight into which professors may be preferential because of their teaching style or test difficulty. There are also numerous sites to read feedback about college courses and instructors. I have provided sample semester schedules for your first two years on this page and the next that is similar to the path that I took. This can easily be adapted depending on your specific requirements and goals.

Freshmen Year

Fall Semester	Spring Semester	Summer Semester
Biology I: 4 cr.	Biology II: 4 cr.	Physics I: 4 cr.
Animal Science I: 4 cr.	Chemistry I: 4 cr.	
Required Math- College Algebra / Calculus: 3 cr.	Veterinary Science: 3 cr.	
General Ed / Electives: 4-6 cr.	General Ed / Electives: 4-7 cr.	
Total Credit Hours: 15-17	Total Credit Hours: 15-18	Total Credit Hours: 4

Sophomore Year

Fall Semester	Spring Semester	Summer Semester
Chemistry II: 4 cr.	Organic Chemistry: 5 cr.	General Ed / Electives: 3-6 Cr.
Physics II: 4 cr.	Genetics: 4 cr.	
Microbiology: 4 cr.	Business Class: 3 cr.	
General Ed / Electives: 3-6 cr.	General Ed / Electives: 3-6 cr.	
Total Credit Hours: 15-18	Total Credit Hours: 15-18	Total Credit Hours: 3-6

By completing courses in a similar fashion as above, you will be well positioned to finish the pre-requisites for veterinary school by the end of your third year, while still balancing some easier elective and general education courses each semester. I would consider utilizing the summer semester to help maintain good academic progress, but it is optional. A good strategy may be to take just one of your more difficult courses during the summer so you can give it your undivided attention.

The summer semester is about half as long as the fall or spring semester, so the classroom time is condensed more heavily during the term. You will be in a class roughly twice as many hours per week as you would during a normal semester. For example, a 3 credit hour lecture course would have 3 hours of lecture time per week during the spring or fall, but 6 hours per week during a the summer term. Therefore, it may not be a good idea to take a heavy course load (more than 6 credit hours) during the summer.

Additionally, many scholarships do not extend aid to cover summer courses, so may need to be paid for out of pocket or with loans. Finally, the summer break is a good opportunity to accrue a lot of veterinary experience hours. You may not be able to work a ton of hours into your schedule during the school year, and it is probably a good idea to focus on school entirely the first semester or two until you have adjusted to college coursework. Therefore, you may want to take just one class or take the summer off school entirely to open your schedule for obtaining as much veterinary experience as possible.

You might have noticed some of my recommendations for elective courses in the sample schedule above. Depending on your major, some of these classes may be required for you, particularly if you are majoring in animal science. Animal Science I and Veterinary Science were options within my organismal biology major to take as required electives. I would have taken them regardless, but it was nice that they also counted in some way towards my degree rather than as pure electives. I also later took a farm animal physiology course that was helpful as well for my veterinary knowledge base. All three of these animal science courses helped me by introducing information that was covered in one or more courses later during veterinary school.

I would recommend some business courses as well, especially if you think there might be any chance that you would be part or sole owner of a veterinary practice someday. Even if you don't think practice ownership is for you, I feel that all veterinarians should have some business knowledge. Part of being a valuable employee to the practice owner is understanding the overall business concept, how you fit in, and how to maximize your value to the practice. The more valuable you are to the practice, the more you should earn in salary and benefits.

I also believe that an individual is not able to make an educated decision on whether or not they desire to be a practice owner or if they would be a successful one until they have been a practicing veterinarian for at least a couple of years. I know many practice owners who believed that they did not want to own a practice or would not be successful owners until several years after becoming veterinarians. Practice owners generally have higher salaries than non-owners, known as associates. With practice ownership, you also are building net worth in a significant asset (the practice and potentially the real estate) that should increase in value over time, sometimes greatly increase in value depending on how well you manage it. This asset can be sold when you are ready to retire and make up a significant portion of your nest egg for a comfortable retirement.

Some people may not agree with me on the importance of business classes. I recommend that you should consider your personal situation and if you can fit them into your schedule while still reaching your academic goals such as applying to veterinary school early or graduating on time. If you determine that some business classes fit into your plans, in addition to a general business course, I would also recommend an accounting or a small business class. You are not trying to become an accounting expert, but a background in the terminology and concepts will help you when working with your accountant and allow you to do some of your own analysis. Veterinary clinics are generally small businesses. Principles covered in a small business course such as different business structures, management principles, and tax implications are applicable on a daily basis for veterinarians.

There are still other courses that can be useful in veterinary school. Depending on your major, they may or may not be considered electives. My college had a comparative vertebrate anatomy course in the Biology department that covered the functional anatomy of all vertebrates (animal species with backbones). In the laboratory sessions, we dissected and studied the anatomical structures of the shark, turtle, bird, salamander, and cat. This course covered some of the same information as my veterinary school anatomy class and was taught in a very similar style. Needless to say, taking that course was beneficial in both getting into veterinary school and performing well in my veterinary school anatomy course.

Biology courses in animal physiology are also highly recommended. Additionally, any veterinary-focused courses your school may offer should be strongly considered. Not all schools offer very many of these types of courses, but they are likely to introduce concepts that will give you a leg up in veterinary school. There was even one class at my veterinary school that undergraduate students could take with veterinary students. Later, when they were veterinary students, they did not have to take the course and had that four extra hours of down time each week to study while the rest of us were in class. With one less class to study and prepare for, this really lightened their course load for that term.

The final thing to consider when choosing your courses each semester is the total number of credit hours you are taking. To maintain steady academic progress, I would suggest taking 15 credit hours at a minimum. Some veterinary schools evaluate the average number of hours each candidate has taken per semester, and factor it into your overall rating. Veterinary school curriculums can progress at a pace equivalent to as much as 20-24 credit hours per semester, which is a very tough course load.

Admissions committees look more favorably on students who have taken 17 or 18 credit hours consistently than one who averaged less than 15 credit hours per semester because they are more proven with a higher workload. Of course, your extra-curricular activities may necessitate taking a smaller course load and, in this case, an explanation in your essays or interview can overcome any disadvantage. The bottom line is that you should take as many credit hours as you can handle while still balancing your relevant extracurricular activities. Do not overextend yourself at the expense of your GPA, but be sure to challenge yourself somewhat to help prepare for the veterinary school course load.

Extra-curricular activity options in college are endless, especially at some of the larger schools. There are clubs, organizations, and activities for just about any interest, hobby, or talent. The college melting pot is a prime environment for you to forge friendships and memories that will last a lifetime. As much as college has to offer, be sure to continue to place a priority activities that will help secure your dream of becoming a veterinarian and set you up for future success. Be an active member of the pre-veterinary club and consider taking a leadership role. Gaining membership to an honor society is also a nice addition to your application and can help you build connections with other students and successful alumni.

Most importantly, continue to build on your veterinary experience by obtaining as many observation hours as possible in a variety of types of veterinary practices. Back in the high school chapter, I discussed obtaining these observation hours in depth, and if for some reason you skipped that chapter or you need a refresher please go back and review this information under the "Extra-curricular Activities" section. As I mentioned in that section, the number of hours of experience a student has obtained can play a big role in whether or not they are accepted into veterinary school.

Most schools have a minimum number of hours that all candidates must have, but the majority of students that are accepted greatly exceed the minimum requirement, with well over 1,000 hours of experience. Veterinary schools still train students in both Large and Small animal medicine, so it is critical to gain experience by observing veterinarians working with Dogs, Cats, Horses, and Cattle. Additional experience with Exotic animals, animal research, and animal shelters is helpful as well, and as mentioned previously, can help set you apart from other applicants.

Strive to gain as much experience as possible, it will help your chances with admission and build a useful knowledge base for both classroom and clinical success in veterinary school. There is simply no substitute for quality, first-hand experience. You can learn all about a disease process or procedure, but seeing a disease in a clinical setting or gaining hands on experience performing that procedure really helps to bring the whole picture together. Be sure to check with upper classmen about their experiences with clinics in the area, and which cater to pre-veterinary students the best by offering quality observation time and hands-on experience. Obtaining a job at one of these clinics can be a golden opportunity to gain experience while also earning money. This is a more efficient use of your time compared to working a separate part time job in fast food or retail and still having to get volunteer hours.

Even if you don't necessarily need the money in college, try to fit a job into your schedule. Veterinary school is expensive; having some money in savings will definitely come in handy during that time when it is difficult to impossible to find time to work. Any savings you have will decrease your post-graduation student debt load. As I have stated time and time again, that always needs to be at the front of your mind. You will thank yourself later when your classmates have student loans adding up to more than their mortgage. Some of these individuals may still be paying on their loans when their *children* are in college. This is not a position you want to be in.

I can speak from experience here, my student loan debt is definitely is a major impact on my budget every month. I am aggressively working to pay my loans back, and they will be long gone by the time my children heading off to college, but I am not able to save as much for my retirement as I would like, drive that nice new car, or go on a dream vacation that we could potentially afford without that student loan payment.

I don't regret my decision to go to veterinary school and incur student debt in the process. I just wish I had made some more adjustments along the way that might have decreased the final bill somewhat. Take my suggestions and continuously track the total cost of your education (Tuition + Living Expenses) and consider it in every purchase decision you make. I once heard a saying that I feel rings very true "Choose to live like a *doctor* while you are a *student* and you will have to live like a *student* while you are a *doctor.*"

College Benchmarks/Goals: When setting goals to reach during your college career, knowing the academic profile of the typical student accepted to veterinary school is very useful. You may have already obtained this information while researching your college choices. In that chapter, under the pre-veterinary track record section, I suggested obtaining any information that some prospective veterinary school(s) make available about the incoming class for that year.

At this point, it is not necessary to have a definitive list of which veterinary schools to which you will apply, but you do need to identify the school(s) in which you are likely to apply so that you can obtain the information necessary to set your college benchmarks. We will cover which veterinary schools you should apply to in more detail in the next. If you are unsure, you can at least get a basic idea of your most likely schools checking with other students on campus or faculty advisers.

Once you have identified some prospective veterinary schools, look for information about the most recent incoming class on their websites. Some schools list demographical information such as age, undergraduate major, average GPA, average GRE or MCAT score, etc. If this information is not available online, try contacting the veterinary school, they may have the information you seek, or an admissions adviser may be able to give you some targets as far as veterinary experience, GPA, and GRE or MCAT scores.

Set your goals based on the information you can gather. At a minimum, you should strive to achieve at a level consistent with the *Average Accepted Student* to your prospective veterinary school(s) in all areas that are evaluated during the application process. If you fit the profile of the typical student accepted each year, then most likely, you will receive strong consideration for admission and have a good chance of being accepted. However, remember that every year there are students who are not accepted that meet or even exceed these benchmarks.

Therefore, to maximize your chances, you should set your goals as high as possible, but also within reason. Avoid goals with a low likelihood of success, or cause stress, anxiety, or pressure, most individuals do not thrive when dealing with these burdens. As in high school, develop smaller, short term goals that build up to your larger, long term aspirations. This helps build confidence along the way as well as keeps you on a track to optimize your chances of getting into veterinary school. For example, set goals each semester for grades in some of your more challenging courses and overall GPA for the term.

Don't forget about goal setting with your pre-veterinary experience as well. Also target obtaining other honors such as leadership positions in your extra-curricular activities and other achievements to boost your veterinary school application.

When the time comes to apply to veterinary school, you don't want to be worried, thinking "Have I done enough?" To put your best foot forward during interviews, you need to have the confidence that you have yourself in the best position possible and simply need to take the next step in the process to realize your dream. By setting and reaching your goals during your college career, you can move on to the application process with this confidence and maximize your odds of success.

Getting into Veterinary School: The Application Process

If you have made it this far in your journey, you are in the home stretch! The veterinary school application process is where you will make your final push into veterinary school. In this chapter, we will cover the application timeline, help you decide which school(s) you will apply to, go over each section of the Veterinary Medical College Application Service (VMCAS), and discuss how to ace the interview process.

Application Timeline (see figure on next page): The application process starts in May or June of the year PRIOR to your application. Application deadlines are usually in the fall, with some supplemental application components such as your fall grades due after the conclusion of the fall semester. Interviews are usually in the late winter/early spring and acceptance letters are sent out later in the spring. This is just a rough guideline, with most schools having a timeline within these parameters. Be sure to verify the timeline with each of your target schools. A missed deadline generally results in an automatic rejection.

Pre-Application	May-June	September-October	December-January	February-March	March-May
Draft list of Schools you will Apply to	Application Process Opens--- Start Early!	Application Due	Additional Application Materials Due	Interviews	Acceptance Letters & Packets Sent Out

Choosing Your Veterinary School(s): The first step in the application process is deciding on the schools to which you will apply. In general, if you are a resident of a state where a veterinary school is located, your best chances of acceptance are through applying to that veterinary school. Your odds of acceptance may be so much higher with that one school that it may not be worthwhile applying to other schools. Each application you submit costs money, and the costs can really add up if you applying to a lot of schools. Also, remember that the difference between in-state tuition and what you would pay by going to an out of state veterinary school can be upwards of $100,000 or more, essentially doubling the cost of your veterinary education. Therefore, it is usually best for a student to give priority to attending the veterinary school located in their resident state.

However, there are exceptions to this case. Highly populated states like New York and California have veterinary schools located within their state, (California has two) but the demand still greatly outpaces the availability of seats for in-state students. Students in these states often apply to many out of state schools as well as their in-state options. If you happen to be a resident of a state that does not have a veterinary school, check and see if your state has an agreement with any veterinary schools to accept a certain number of students from your state. If any such arrangements exist, definitely plan on applying to those schools among many others to maximize your chances of being accepted.

In the event you are accepted to multiple schools, you get to choose which one you will attend; no harm in that! If you are applying to several out of state schools, do some research to determine if some offer the ability to obtain in state residency status during your time there, which would allow you to gain access to the lower in-state tuition rates. At the time of publishing, my alma mater, the University of Missouri College of Veterinary Medicine allowed out of state students to obtain in state residency if they met certain requirements. There may be other veterinary schools who offer this perk as well, and I recommend having each of these schools on your list if you are looking at out of state options.

VMCAS Veterinary School Application: As stated in the chart above, you should have the list of schools you will be applying to before the applications open online in May and June. Deadlines for submission of Application components vary some from school to school, so having your list up front will allow you to make sure you get everything sent in on time. As of 2013, nearly every U.S. veterinary school used VMCAS as the portal by which to submit applications.

The trend in recent years has been for schools to move their applications to this service, and all schools may utilize VMCAS in the near future. On their website, you can access the portal to fill out the primary veterinary school application that will be submitted to each of your target schools.

Their website (aavmc.org) also has tons of information on the application process and details for each and every school such as deadlines, tuition rates, class size, etc. for the upcoming admissions cycle. I highly recommend browsing their website to see what they have to offer. It is updated regularly, giving you the most current information. In addition to the general application, most schools also require a supplemental application to be submitted, which can be accessed at links posted on the VMCAS website under the link "Supplemental Application Chart" or at each school's own website. Some schools don't allow you to access their supplemental application until you have submitted your VMCAS application, so be sure to get started and complete your VMCAS application early.

Through the VMCAS application portal, first select the schools in which you will be applying to under the "Designations" link. Next, start the application by entering basic information about yourself and your parents such as contact information, race/ethnicity, where you went to high school, colleges you have attended, current student status, current college GPA, and college courses taken and the corresponding grades you earned. You will need to submit official transcripts that go directly from your school's registrar's office to the VMCAS. It is recommended that you have your transcripts sent in as early as they are available after your latest term to allow time for processing and verification. Keep in mind that the deadline for transcript submission to VMCAS is about a month earlier than the deadline for completion of your application.

The application also requires information about standardized tests you have already taken or plan to take such as the GRE and/or MCAT. I would rely on your pre-veterinary advisor or an advisor from your preferred veterinary school when deciding which test to take. I know the selection formula when I applied to veterinary school at the University of Missouri favored the GRE over the MCAT, but this difference was very slight, and not necessarily significant. Tests change, selection criteria and preferences change almost yearly, so I wouldn't get too hung up on which one you take. Again, rely on your advisor(s) to help steer you in this situation. However, I definitely recommend spending a significant amount of time preparing for these tests. Each school places a different amount of weight on them, but every part of your admissions profile is important.

Like the ACT or SAT, the best way to prepare for these exams is to master material as you are exposed to it in college, but spending time focusing on additional test prep material specific to each exam can be very helpful. There are tons of resources online and in-print to help you prepare. There are even preparatory courses, which can be expensive, but could be vital if you need a little extra boost to your test scores. As with the standardized tests in high school, take your graduate exams early, allowing for additional attempts if necessary. Also remember that you will not be allowed to submit scores from exams taken after a certain date, with the exact deadline varying depending on the school. Failure to take and/or submit scores from required exams prior to a school's deadline generally results in an automatic rejection.

The next section of the application covers your work experience, with separate sections for your veterinary experience, general animal experience, experience in research activities, and other employment experience. To be considered veterinary experience, the work must be related to animals and be under the supervision of a veterinary health professional. Experience involving animals but not under veterinary supervision is considered animal experience. This is where the logs you have been keeping become very useful. Otherwise you will have to estimate based on your memory, which can either be too low (hurting your application) or overestimate your experience (dishonest and unethical=bad karma, you don't want bad karma). For veterinary experience, you should include any time spent at a veterinary clinic when a veterinarian was present.

General animal experience is not viewed as highly as veterinary experience but still has value. Some individuals that grew up on a farm or have been otherwise involved with animals over the course of their lives will often have lots of hours to list here. Having a log of your animal experience will also help with this step, especially as some individuals will have many different experiences to report.

The veterinary profession is steadily becoming more and more involved in various research fields, and the need for veterinarians in research continues to grow. Therefore any experience you have in research will be favorable as well. Finally, don't forget to submit any work experience not already listed. Some students are unable to find paid positions that provide veterinary, animal, or research experience and obtain most of their hours as volunteers. If you were able to both volunteer and hold a job, this shows that you have good time management skills. The admissions committee generally likes to see well-rounded individuals that can succeed while balancing school, work, and volunteering because these students are more likely to succeed under the increased weight of the veterinary school workload.

Next you need to provide information about your community activities and Honors or Awards. Be as detailed as possible and be sure not to forget any of your awards or activities. Some very busy individuals may participate in lots of activities and forget about the charity event they helped with or an award they received. To avoid forgetting something on your application, try one or more brainstorming sessions prior to filling out each section. Dedicate a notebook to your application, and have a page for each section of the application. Sit down several times and try to list each item required in that section. Keep your notebook with you so you can write down things you think of when on the go. I know I do some of my best brainstorming during solo meals or when I am driving. (Of course, don't write WHILE you are driving)

At this point you might be asking "I haven't had to write an essay yet!" Don't worry, the VMCAS requires one under the "Personal Statement" section. This section provides a prompt for which the student provides a lengthy (~5000 word) response. A sample prompt I saw asked the student to describe their interests, activities and experiences in veterinary medicine and expand by discussing how they have prepared the student for a professional program. In addition, the prompt asked the applicant to discuss their understanding of the veterinary profession as a whole and your career interests, goals, and objectives.

Another common essay or interview question is "Why did you choose this career?" This can be a bit of a trap question, admissions committee members are not impressed by responses based on central ideas such as "I always loved animals" or "I don't like dealing with people but love animals". I know these seem like natural responses, but they want to see that you are driven by more than just a love for animals, that this is your *calling*.

Take time on your essay, carefully constructing it, proofreading it, and having others proofread and critique the document. Treat it as if it were going to be published in a prominent magazine. Make sure it is as detailed and as well written as possible, as well as completely free of misspellings and other errors that could distract the reader from your message.

The final component of your application is external evaluations. You are required to have at least 3 evaluators submit references electronically through the online VMCAS electronic reference portal. You can list up to 6 evaluators, but be sure to confirm that each individual is willing to provide a letter of reference on your behalf prior to listing them on your application. I would suggest selecting a variety of evaluators. Several of your evaluators should be veterinarians, but also get references from academic advisors or faculty leaders of college organizations. I would even have a personal reference or two from a neighbor, high school teacher, or prominent member of your community.

Your evaluators should be familiar with your work ethic and personal characteristics so they can provide quality insight and paint a positive picture about you for the admissions committee. Brief each evaluator on the process of how to submit the reference and be sure to emphasize the deadline. Consider having an earlier "soft" deadline to make sure all references are received by VMCAS well in advance of the final deadline. Finally, be sure to send a "Thank You" card to your evaluators for taking the time to provide an evaluation for you. You can submit your application prior when your references are received, but your application will not be considered complete until at least three references have been submitted to VMCAS.

Now that your application is complete, proofread it several times. I would suggest having another person proofread it as well. You must make your application payment prior to submitting your application. The cost will depend on which schools you are applying to. Once your application is submitted, print a copy of your completed application and your confirmation page. Remember that you will have to request transcripts from each college or university you have attended to be sent to VMCAS, but test scores have to be sent directly to each of your designated veterinary schools.

Once you have completed and submitted your VMCAS application, your work is not done. Most schools require candidates to complete supplemental applications. If you are applying to many schools, these will take a significant amount of time to complete. You will probably be providing some of the same information on each one, but there is likely to be differences as well, such as essay topics or other interview questions. Budget your time wisely and keep yourself on track to complete all the required work well in advance of the deadlines. You don't want to be in a rush at any point in the application process, a simple mistake here or there can reflect poorly, or if an important detail or deadline is missed, it could disqualify you completely from admission that year.

After all the applications, tests, and deadlines, it will seem like there is a bit of a lull in the admissions process. Use this break in the action to have a very strong fall semester. Grades from this term will be your last chance to leave an impression with your academic abilities. Most applicants at this point are juniors or seniors, usually taking some of the most challenging courses in their degree program.

Earning excellent grades despite a difficult course load will stand out to admissions committee members. It indicates that you are better prepared for the veterinary school curriculum. As I stated earlier, some schools even place special weight in their admissions formulas on the students' GPA in the most recent two or three semesters. Around the end of the fall term there are another set of deadlines. Grades from the fall semester need to be submitted and some schools have deadlines around this time for submission of additional application materials.

Additionally, you should continue to gain veterinary experience after submitting your application. Focus specifically on areas that you are lacking in such as Small Animal, Large Animal, Exotics, etc. Some schools will ask about additional veterinary experience you have accrued since submitting your application. Sometimes these hours will be added to your total number of hours, providing an extra boost for your application!

Interviews: The time for visiting your prospective schools (if you haven't already) and meeting with the admissions committee is here! During your visit, be sure to get a thorough tour of the veterinary school facilities and try to take in as much as you can about the community. Try to evaluate what your housing options would be (is it a nice area that is safe?) as well as if conveniences are located nearby (grocery stores etc.) In the event you are accepted to multiple schools, you want to have an idea which school presents the best fit for you.

Be sure to take detailed notes while visiting each school and surrounding community. Pictures can also be very helpful. If you are visiting several schools in a relatively short period of time, they may blend together. Having visual cues from each place can help you better recall each one and organize your thoughts when deciding the best fit for you.

Interviews are held at different times for each school, but they generally start in January and run through March or April. The interview is your last chance to make an impression on the admissions committee. The interview carries a varying amount of weight in each school's selection criteria, but is always critical, so you need to be on point for your interview. This is where the admissions committee members get to attach a face and a voice to the application in front of them, YOURS!

Most people would agree that interviews of any sort make them nervous and uncomfortable. These feelings are intensified when you are interviewing with your dream of becoming a veterinarian on the line. To be a bit nervous is only normal, but you cannot allow your anxiety to negatively affect your performance. You need to go into the interview with un-wavering confidence and composure, which you can develop by properly preparing for your interview.

One of the best ways to improve your interview skills is to perform "mock" interviews. Some veterinary schools may make sample interview questions available. Also, if you know any current veterinary students or students who applied the year before, rely on any information they might have about their interview. Have friends, family, and your college advisor(s) ask questions and practice relaying a thoughtful and concise answer with clarity and confidence. Be sure to also have them make up questions on the fly to keep you on your toes. Finally, be sure to keep up with major events and changes occurring within the veterinary industry. You may be asked about some of the current events in veterinary medicine during your interview.

Realize that it is unlikely that you will be able to practice all or even a majority of the questions that the admissions committee could ask in an interview. However, by working through many mock interviews, you will become more comfortable with developing quality responses on the fly, which will pay dividends in your interview with the admissions committee. As the saying goes, "Practice makes perfect."

While mock interviews can help build your interview experience and confidence, you must also prepare psychologically. There are many reasons I highly recommend applying to veterinary school before your senior year, but I think it helps you psychologically in your interview in two ways. First, if you are applying as a sophomore or junior, you literally can go into that interview relaxed, with nothing to lose. If you aren't accepted you can continue to work on your degree and apply again next year. When your interview the next year comes around you will have the added learning experience and confidence from interviewing the year before.

There is no doubt that the interview is important. I am not trying to state otherwise. The interview may even be the final deciding factor for students on the proverbial admissions "bubble". However, you must block out these thoughts and avoid putting pressure on yourself. Go into your interview relaxed and confident, prepared to simply do your best and let the cards fall as they will, because you will be fine either way. Applying early to veterinary school and following my previous advice to identify a viable fallback career path will help you reach the necessary state of mind to ace your interview.

Closing Thoughts

I know what you are thinking. "You mean there is no Vet School chapter?!, the book printer must have accidentally omitted it, I should give them a call..." Sorry folks, no dedicated, step-by-step veterinary school chapter, but just stick with me here as I explain. I want to start with a quote that I heard within an hour of stepping into the College of Veterinary Medicine at the University of Missouri. It was said by Dr. Ron Cott, the Dean of Student Affairs, and he borrowed it from Anthony Robbins, a well-known motivational speaker and self-improvement guru.

Dr. Cott was trying to ease the anxiety of members of our incoming class about making it through veterinary school and I think it is a great rule to live by, and can function as a mantra of sorts. "Do what you've always done and you will get what you've always gotten." The quote is both extremely true and concise, but the best part is that it applies perfectly to you, the reader of this book.

If you read this book, followed its principles, stuck to my advice, and are accepted into veterinary school, that means you fully applied yourself to your goals that were derived through research and strategic thinking. By doing these things and maximizing your chances of getting into veterinary school, you have developed most, if not all of the personal qualities and tools needed to succeed in veterinary school.

Just getting into veterinary school requires intense focus, time management, prioritization, good study skills/habits, and mental and (sometimes) physical fortitude. I am not going to lie, veterinary school is likely to be more difficult in many regards than anything you have ever done up to that point, and you may have to raise your game. But if you have developed the necessary tools and skills to make it that far, you just have to continue to build in these areas to reach your full potential.

Veterinary school tested me in ways that I had expected, but in many more areas than I had could have ever imagined, and I am much better and stronger for it. I think most of my colleagues would agree. You could probably write a how-to-guide on individual classes in veterinary school, and you will be spending long hours in class and even longer hours studying outside of class the first few years of veterinary school.

Every school is different, but most schools have two and a half to three years of training in the classroom and in labs where you develop your veterinary knowledge base and skills. During the classroom phase, you will be taking a course load equivalent to 20-24+ college credit hours. There are semesters where you are receiving instruction in class and in lab 40+ hours per week. That's before you get to your time spent studying, which will be significant. I don't know that I kept real close track, but most veterinary students spend an additional 20-40 hours or more per week studying.

The final phase, clinical training, lasts the remaining 12 to 18 months prior to graduation. This is where you essentially work as a veterinarian in a clinical setting, under the supervision of experts in each segment of veterinary medicine who advise and assist you in applying what you have learned and reinforcing these principles with real clients and patients. This gives you the experience and confidence to function as a veterinarian on an entry level as you begin your career after graduation.

The clinical phase often requires students to work long and sometimes odd hours such as overnights or in an on-call capacity. It is not always glamorous, you will probably at one point or another perform all functions from janitorial and kennel work to functioning as a technician at times, as well as taking a primary role in management of your own cases while receiving advisement from veterinary experts in fields such as Internal Medicine, Ophthalmology, Surgery, Neurology, Emergency and Critical Care, Oncology, Equine Medicine and Surgery, and Food Animal Medicine and Surgery.

Amazingly, you will still manage to find time for yourself, and it is important to do so in order to keep your sanity. You will also develop close bonds with your classmates, and these people will be integral as study partners as well as for social activities outside of school to step away and get a release from the daily grind. You might drift apart from some of these people after graduation due to time or distance, but others will continue to be among your closest friends as you go through your career and life.

Some individuals manage to hold a job at times during veterinary school and it amazes me. I had some odd jobs here and there to make some money, but nothing requiring a significant number of hours on a consistent basis. My daughter was born 3 months before I started veterinary school and my son came in the middle of my 18 months of clinical training.

Our little family was my outlet and escape from the rigors of veterinary school. My wife worked full time, sacrificing the opportunity to stay home with our children, who went to daycare. In the evening, she had to be super-mom, at times functioning as a single parent because vet school kept me occupied both day and night. Everyone in our family made sacrifices for me to become a veterinarian, and we got through it together, galvanizing us and making us a stronger family unit. Particularly, the bond my wife and I share from our experience.

Even if you don't have a spouse or significant other as you go through vet school, your classmates function as a surrogate family. As you near the end of your training and reach graduation, you realize how important this group of people was. You weren't close to everyone, but worked closely with almost every person at one time or another. Over the course of four years, you develop a connection with your classmates, a strong sense of "We got through this together."

At the end of it all, you will have a sense of pride and accomplishment unlike any you have ever experienced. There is no other feeling like it, walking across that stage and getting your diploma. It is a culmination of many years of hard work and sacrifice, and a part of you finally feels complete. I can assure you that it is all worth it in the end. I love my job, and don't see any end to that feeling. If I won the lottery, I would still choose to work as a veterinarian in some capacity. I think most of my fellow veterinarians would say the same.

Regardless of where you are on the path to becoming to a veterinarian, whether you are just starting out, in high school, or a college student well on your way, you have some real work ahead of you. Learn from and apply what you have read in this book and never stop pushing towards your dream. Before long, you will find yourself walking into a veterinary school somewhere and in that moment, say to yourself "Do what I've always done, and I will get what I've always gotten" and realize that you will be just fine.

ABOUT THE AUTHOR

Dr. Zachary Patterson grew up in Pleasant Hill, Missouri, a small town near Kansas City. He sparked an interest in animal health while spending time with his grandfather who raised cattle and was further inspired by the local veterinarians who were well regarded and respected by the local community.

After graduating from Pleasant Hill High School in 2004, Dr. Patterson received his undergraduate training at Missouri State University in Springfield, Missouri and majored in Biology. Once he had completed the required courses, he received early acceptance at the University of Missouri College of Veterinary Medicine after his junior year of college. After four years of classroom, laboratory, and clinical training, he graduated in 2011 and joined Blake Veterinary Hospital, a busy practice in Dade City, Florida which is near Tampa.

In March 2014, Dr. Patterson accepted the opportunity to return to his hometown to become an owner at Pleasant Hill Animal Clinic and realize his dream of owning a veterinary practice. Dr. Patterson's professional interests include client education, surgery, and emergency/critical care medicine. He aspires to own and raise livestock using sustainable methods and has an interest in real estate investing. He is married to his high school sweetheart Melissa, and is the proud father of Aliceyn and Benson.

A Final Thanks to You, the Reader

I would like to give my most sincere thanks for reading my book. I hope it provides guidance and helps you reach your dream of becoming a veterinarian. The biggest compliment I can receive is when a reader recommends my book to someone else, gives a favorable review on Amazon, or likes us on facebook. Thank you again for reading my book and I wish the best luck in your journey to become a veterinarian.

We can be found on facebook at:
www.facebook.com/howtobecomeaveterinarian